Wonderscience

A developmentally appropriate guide
to hands-on science for young children.

by

Wendy Nichols & Kimberly Nichols

Published by:
Learning Expo Publishing
5420 S. Espana Ct.
Aurora, CO 80015

Library of Congress Catalog Card Number 90-60081

ISBN 0-9625907-0-3

First Printing 1990
Second Printing 1992
Third Printing 1995

Printed in the United States of America

Dedication

To our parents, Richard and Diane
for their love, patience and encouragement.

Introduction

This is not another bean sprouts and bird feeder science book! We've put together projects designed to give you a new angle on science. Each project is formulated to allow the child to hypothesize, experiment, observe and verify. Our hands-on science emphasizes learning as an interactive process.

Table of Contents

Forces & Movement

Sound

Air

Water

Light

Forces and Movement

Floating Paper Clip

Materials: Paper Clip
           Coffee Can
           Masking Tape
           Lightweight Thread
           Magnet

Presentation:

1. Attach the magnet across the diameter of the coffee can with masking tape. The magnet should be over the edge.
2. Place the can on the table.
3. Tie thread to one end of the paper clip.
4. Place the paper clip on the under side of the magnet until it is suspended in mid air.
5. Tape excess thread to table.

Open Ended Question:

1. How can the paper clip stand up by itself?
2. What happens to the paper clip if you take the can and magnet away?

Variations:

1. Putting items between the magnet and the paper clip, i.e., paper, fingers.
2. Blow on the magnet. (You can't knock it down.)

Notes: No need to be gentle with this project. It is sturdy and easily reconstructed.

Dancing Magnet

Materials: Table Tops
                          Two Small Chairs
                          String
                          Two Magnets
                          Rod, Dowel, or Broom Handle
                          Masking Tape

Presentation:
1. Support the rod between the backs of two chairs.
2. Secure the rod with masking tape.
3. Tie the end of the string to the magnet and the other end to the rod.
4. The magnet should hang 6 - 12 inches above the table.
5. Take the second magnet and wave rapidly back and forth in front of the first magnet.
6. With practice, the magnet will begin to spin rapidly in a circle.

Open Ended Question:
1. How did you make the magnet move?
2. What can you do to make the magnet move a different way?

Variations:
1. With varying movements from the hand-held magnet, the dancing magnet changes direction.
2. Use additional metal objects (i.e., paper clips, bolts, screws, etc.) to attract and repel the magnet.

Crazy Roller

Materials: Small wide can
Clay
Blocks

Presentation:
1. Cover rim of can with duct tape. (Will prevent cuts and give can traction.)
2. Place clay inside of can. It should cover approx. 1/3 of the can.
3. Press clay firmly to secure it in place.
4. Make a slightly angled plane with blocks (see photo).
5. Place clay side of can uphill (see photo).
6. Roll can.

Open Ended Question:
1. Why does the can go up the hill?
2. What does the clay do to the can?

Variations:
1. Rolling can across the floor.

Plexiglass with Magnets

Materials: Sheet of Plexiglass (4' x 2' or larger)
Magnet
Various metal objects like metal cars, paper clips, washers, nuts, etc.

Presentation:
1. Place plexiglass between two chairs.
2. Position child with a magnet under plexiglass.
3. Place metal objects on top of plexiglass.
4. Allow child to experiment.

Open Ended Question:
1. How did you make that move? (Point to object.)

Variations:
1. Instead of metal objects try filings.
2. Use non-metal and metal objects and allow the child to differentiate between the two.

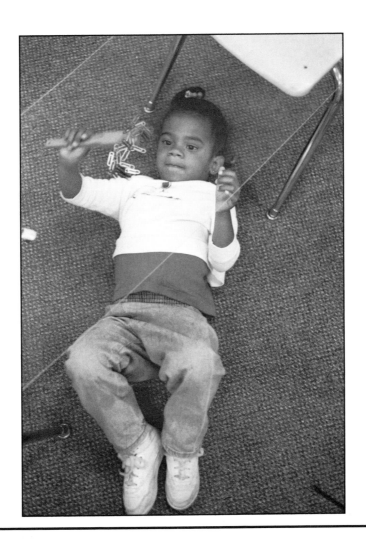

Pulley Power

Materials:

Two pulleys
Cord
2 Hooks or 2 Nails
Duct Tape
Clothespins

Presentation:

1. Secure one pulley with hook or nail to a wall.
2. Thread cord through both pulleys.
3. Connect cord together with duct tape.
4. Secure second pulley to another wall.
5. Supply clothespins so children may attach items to the cord, i.e., berry baskets, notes, etc.
6. Pull one side of the cord to move items along the transport line.

Open Ended Question:

1. What can you move from here to there?
2. How did you make it move?
3. What other things can you move?

Variations:

1. Vary heights and slopes.

Magnet Marker

Materials:

Marker
Nut
1/2" Washer
Duct Tape
Plexiglass
Paper
Scotch Tape
Blocks
Magnet

Presentation:

1. Place marker through the nut.
2. Place nut and marker on top of the washer so that the marker tip is exposed.
3. Secure marker, washer and nut together with duct tape.
4. Place plexiglass on top of stacks of blocks (3 or 4 on each side).
5. Scotch tape paper to plexiglass.
6. Place marker on paper.
7. Move magnet underneath the plexiglass to begin drawing.

Open Ended Question:

1. How are you making this drawing?

Notes:

Make sure the washer lies flat against the plexiglass. Duct tape should only cover the top side of the washer.

Color Wheel

Materials:
9 volt battery
Miniature motor
Cork 1-1/2" in diameter
Push Pin
Paper in various colors
Duct Tape
1 block

Presentation:
1. Secure motor to edge of the block with tape.
2. The spinning part of the motor should project past the end of the block.
3. Secure battery to block behind the motor. (The motor's wires should easily reach the battery.)
4. Make a small hole in the center of the cork with push pin.
5. Remove push pin.
6. Put the spinning component of the motor in the hole you just made with the pin.
7. Cut a circle of light weight paper approx. 7" in diameter. Paper should be 2 or more colors.
8. Attach the paper to the cork with the push pin.
9. Connect wires to battery.
10. Watch colors blend and change as the motor spins the color wheel.

Open Ended Question:
1. How did you make the colors change?
2. What makes the paper spin?

Variations:
Multi-colored paper.

Launch Pad

Materials:

Long thin block
Large round block
Duct tape
Paper towels

Presentation:

1. Wad paper towels into a ball.
2. Completely cover paper towels in duct tape to form a ball.
3. Secure round block to table with duct tape.
4. Secure long thin block to the round block, leaving one end extended further than the other (see photo).
5. Secure the long block with duct tape along its width.
6. Place the ball on the long end of the long block.
7. Place your hand on the short end of the block.
8. Push down quickly and launch the ball.

Open Ended Question:

1. How did you make the ball do that?
2. What else can you launch?

Variations:

1. Launch various unbreakable objects.
2. Use in water play to make big splashes.

Paper Clip Trains

Materials: Large clear acrylic tube
                        Water
                        Colored paper clips
                        Magnet

Presentation: 1. Fill tube with water.
                        2. Connect approx. 7 paper clips to make a train.
                        3. Make approx. 4 trains.
                        4. Leave some paper clips unattached.
                        5. Insert paper clips into tube.
                        6. Seal the tube.
                        7. Move magnet across the surface of the tube.
                        8. Magnet trains will form and move across the tube.

Open Ended Question: 1. What did you do to make the paper clips move?

Marble Table

Materials:
Bulletin board trim
Marble
Play dough
Masking tape
Plastic pipes and joints
Blocks
Tunnels
Berry baskets

Presentation:
1. Tape bulletin board trim around the entire edge of the table.
2. Supply children with all the above mentioned materials.

Open Ended Question:
1. What can you do with all these things?

Variations:
1. Supply additional items to be used on the table.

Notes:
Make sure to let children set up and thus implement their own play. It can be tempting to give children ideas for inclines, etc. However, building up their own ideas, children will gain a better understanding of the concepts at hand.

Pendulum Play

Materials: String
                    Duct tape
                    Paper towels

Presentation:
1. Wad paper towels into a ball and cover with duct tape.
2. Connect one end of string to ball.
3. Connect other end of string to ceiling.
4. Ball should be suspended at thigh height of child.
5. Swing pendulum to begin play, i.e., knock down towers, playing catch, dodge ball, etc.

Open Ended Question:
1. What can you do with this pendulum?

Stay Away Magnet

Materials:
Two magnets
6" x 10" x 1/2" board (approx.)
3 – 3" wooden dowels
3 nails

Presentation:
1. Place one magnet on the center of the board.
2. Trace around the magnet with a pencil.
3. Remove magnet from board.
4. Mark 2 spots for nail placement on either side of the top of the magnet (see photo).
5. Hammer a nail through the board at each of the 2 top marked spots.
6. Turn the board over to expose the two protruding nails.
7. Place a dowel at the tip of each nail and carefully hammer into place.
8. Position a magnet between dowels while holding the magnet handle.
9. Position the 2nd magnet over the 1st so that they repel each other.
10. Hammer a nail through the holes in the magnet handles.
11. Release hold on magnets.
12. One magnet will float above the other.

Open Ended Question:
1. What are the magnets doing?
2. Why don't the magnets stay together?

Marker Wheel

Materials: Same as Color Wheel on page 8.
                           Markers

Presentation: 1. Same as page 8.
                           2. Paper should be white.
                           3. As wheel turns allow 1st child to gently apply marker.
                           4. Have 2nd child hold wires to battery.

Open Ended Question: 1. What design can you make?
                           2. Why does your picture make circles?

Notes: 1. Thin paper plates work well for this activity.

Salt Pendulum

Materials:
Push pins
Salt
Funnel
Plastic pipes and 4 corner joints
Rope
Blocks
Duct tape
Dark paper
Rubber bands

Presentation:
1. Tape paper to table.
2. Make a square of the pipes and joints.
3. Attach 2 blocks across the square with duct tape (see photo).
4. Secure 2 push pins spaced 2" apart in the center of each block.
5. Anchor rubber bands from push pins.
6. Stretch rubber bands in a crazy eight effect to hold funnel (see photo).
7. Cover the small end of funnell with finger and fill with salt.
8. Take other hand and grasp square.
9. Simultaneously push square in a spinning motion and release funnel.
10. Allow pendulum to move in an uninterrupted pattern.

Open Ended Question:
1. What designs can you make?
2. How can you make the salt fall a different way?

Notes:
For easier clean up cover table with a dark table cloth or sheet.

Magnetize a Spoon

Materials:
Spoon
Magnet
Paper clips or light metal objects.

Presentation:
1. Magnetize a spoon by stroking the spoon continuously in one direction (50–75 times).
2. When stroking, use only one end/pole of the magnet. (Do **not** stroke back and forth.)
3. The spoon should now be magnetized and can pick up light metal objects.

Open Ended Question:
1. How did you make the spoon pick up the paper clip?
2. Why didn't the spoon pick up the paper clip before?

Notes:
1. Let the child experiment with the spoon prior to magnetizing it. (Shows contrast.)

Marble Races

Materials:

Marbles
Board
Blocks
Paint tray (from easel)
Lids (i.e., from tempra paint, mayonnaise jars)

Presentation:

1. Prop board at an angle with blocks under one end.
2. Place opposite end of board in tray.
3. Supply marbles and lids to children.
4. Place marbles underneath lids. (Use varying quantities for different effects.)
5. Roll them down the plane.

Open Ended Question:

1. How do the lids move down the board?
2. What happens when you use 2, (3 & 4) marbles?

Variations:

1. Decorate lids as cars, animals, people, etc.
2. For races (especially with school agers concerned about fairness!) use a ruler so everyone begins at the same time.

One Way Only Box

Materials: Box lid   Large marble   Cardboard   Duct tape

Presentation:
1. Cut a piece of cardboard 1" wider and a 1/2" taller than the width of the box (see photo).
2. Take cardboard and make a pencil line 1/2" in on either side (along the width).
3. Make slits along each line, leaving 1/2" connected at the top of the cardboard.
4. Cut 2 doorways extending from the bottom of the cardboard (the same place you began the slits).
5. Slide cardboard into the middle of the box lid with slits going over the sides (thus securely holding the piece of cardboard over the width of the box).
6. Using the duct tape secure the bottom of the cardboard to the box lid.
7. Cover the doorways with oversized doors (doors should extend past width of doorways).
8. Tape one door over the doorway at the top only.
9. Do the same with the second door but on the opposite side of the piece of cardboard.
10. Marble can travel one way through the doorways.
11. Doorways are one way but in different directions.
12. Children should hold the sides of the box and maneuver marble through doors.

Open Ended Question:
1. How do you make the marble move?
2. How do you get the marble through the doorways?

Static Tube

Materials: Clear acrylic tube
Tiny styrofoam balls
Tissue paper

Presentation:
1. Fill tube with styrofoam balls.
2. With tissue paper vigorously rub tube back and forth.
3. Static will occur.

Open Ended Question:
1. How did you make the balls move?
2. Why are the balls sticking to the top of the tube?

Marker Pendulum

Materials: Same as page 15— Salt Pendulum (exclude salt, funnel, dark paper and rubber bands)
Marker
Butcher paper
Yarn

Presentation:
1. Pendulum (same as page 15).
2. Suspend marker with yarn so it touches paper.
3. Give square a spinning push.
4. Change marker colors for various effects.

Open Ended Question:
1. What designs can you make?
2. How can you make a different design?

Notes:
1. When you originally set up marker, it should hang loosely at an angle at the middle of the paper. This way the marker will remain on the paper when swinging.

The Transporter

Materials:

Pulley
Rope
Clamp
Transport materials: Sand pails, shovels, rakes, etc.

Presentation:

1. Secure one end of rope to wall or fence.
2. Place pulley on rope.
3. Extend rope across sandbox.
4. Secure remaining end of rope to an adjacent wall or fence. Make sure ends of rope are at the same height.
5. Rope should be very taut.
6. Secure clamp to lower portion of pulley (some pulleys come with clamps attached).
7. Attach the pail to the pulley with the clamp.
8. Pail is ready for transport.

Open Ended Question:

1. How did you get the pail from here to there?
2. What else can you transport?

Variations:

1. Angle rope.

Washer Painting

Materials: Blocks
                      Plexiglass
                      Magnet
                      Washer
                      Thread
                      Paint (2 or more colors)
                      Paper
                      Tape

Presentation: 1. Cut 5 or 6 pieces of thread varying in length.
                      2. Tie one end of each thread to the washer.
                      3. Prop the plexiglass on two stacks of blocks.
                      4. Tape a piece of paper on the plexiglass.
                      5. Dip the washer in the paint and place it on the paper.
                      6. Hold magnet **flat** against the bottom of the plexiglass.
                      7. Move magnet to begin painting.
                      8. Continue painting with other colors.

Open Ended Question: 1. How did you make the washer move?
                          2. What is happening to your paper?

Variations: 1. Supply other metallic items to dip in the paint.
                      2. Supply different sizes of washers.

Mini Elevator

Materials:
Berry basket
Large spool (wooden)
Small nail
Large nail
String

Presentation:
1. Tie string to berry basket in the form of an upside-down "Y" (see photo).
2. Secure the remaining end of the string to the spool.
3. Stand the spool on its end and nail the small nail in to form a handle.
4. Nail the large nail into the wall at a right angle. (If nail head is larger than the hole in the middle of the spool, thread the nail through the spool before hammering it in.)
5. With spool on large nail turn handle and you can raise and lower the berry basket.

Open Ended Question:
1. What makes the elevator go up?
2. What makes the elevator go down?
3. Which is faster?

Variations:
1. Let children design an elevator box instead of the berry basket.
2. Supply dramatic play figures.
3. Supply clothespins for notes and drawings.

Sound

Sound Tube

Materials:
Spring (flexible 6" or 7")
2 plastic cups
Cardboard Tube

Presentation:
1. Make sure cups fit into the end of your tube.
2. Take one cup and poke a hole in the bottom.
3. Push one end of spring through the hole until two coils are on the inside of the cup.
4. Place cup in the tube and pull the spring through to the other end of the tube.
5. Poke hole in the 2nd cup and secure spring in the same way.
6. Both cups should fit snugly in each end of the tube.
7. The spring should be stretched between them.
8. Cut a hole in the tube so that children may pluck the spring.
9. Place one end of tube near ear.
10. Pluck the spring for sound effect.

Open Ended Question:
1. What do you hear?
2. How did you make that sound?
3. What other sounds can you make?

Variations:
1. For different sound effects: Shake tube or tap tube with hands or other objects.
2. Decorate tube.

Notes:
If spring ends are sharp, cover with duct tape, caulk or silicon.

Hanging Xylophone

Materials:

Blocks
Plastic pipe and 4 corner joints
Rope
Yarn
Tinker Toy or mallet
1 paper napkin
1 rubber band

Presentation:

1. Construct a rectangle with pipes and joints.
2. Attach rope to each of the four corners.
3. Suspend the rectangle from ceiling so it hangs evenly at child's thigh level.
4. Attach various sized blocks to the rectangle with yarn (see photo).
5. Make a tinker toy mallet and cover the head with the napkin.
6. Secure the napkin with the rubber band.
7. Allow children to create music.

Open Ended Question:

1. What sounds can you make?

Variations:

1. Vary sizes of blocks.

Tube Phone

Materials: 2 Plastic cups
                             Plastic tubing

Presentation: 1. Cut a small hole into the bottom of one cup.
                     2. Make hole a little smaller than the tubing.
                     3. Insert tubing so it is snug.
                     4. Do the same to the other cup.
                     5. Allow first child to talk into cup. (Make sure cup covers entire mouth. Cup should fit up against face.)
                     6. Allow second child to place cup over ear.
                     7. Voices will transmit clearly.

Open Ended Questions: 1. What do you hear?
                             2. How does the sound of your voice go from one cup to the other?

Variations: 1. Have children experiment with phone, i.e., one child indoors and one out, one in the dramatic play area and one in the block area.
                     2. Have children construct phone booth.

Air

Bottle and Balloon

Materials:
Warm Water
Freezer
Bottle
Balloon

Presentation:
1. Place bottle in freezer 1 hour in advance.
2. Blow up the balloon and let the air out (to stretch the balloon).
3. Take the bottle out and place the balloon over the top of the bottle.
4. Place bottle in warm water.
5. Watch as the balloon expands.

Open Ended Question:
1. What is happening to the balloon?
2. What does the warm water do to the cold bottle?

Water Spin

Materials:
Yarn
Clear plastic cup
Colored water
Plastic coffee can lid

Presentation:
1. Punch 3 equidistant holes in the rim of the lid.
2. Tie 3 equal pieces of yarn through the holes. (Yarn should be approx. 2-1/2' long.)
3. Extend yarn to its full length and tie together in one knot (lid should hang evenly).
4. Fill cup with colored water.
5. Place cup in the center of the lid.
6. Spin quickly in a circular motion (avoid jerky movements).

Open Ended Question:
1. Why doesn't the water spill?

Note:
Try out of doors because spills may occur as children practice.

Balloon Spout

Materials:

Plastic bottle (Windex bottle)
Colored water
Balloon

Presentation:

1. Discard spigot on top of plastic bottle.
2. Fill the balloon with water. The water should <u>not</u> cause the balloon to stretch.
3. Empty the balloon water into the bottle.
4. Then add 1/4 cup more water.
5. Place balloon over the mouth of the bottle.
6. Hold upside down until the balloon fills with water.
7. With two hands, squeeze the bottle until all the liquid is pushed into the balloon.
8. Quickly release the pressure on the bottle.
9. Water will spout from the balloon to the top of the bottle.

Open Ended Question:

1. How did you do that?
2. What happens to the balloon?
3. What happens to the water?

Dropping Dropper

Materials:
Clear Plastic tennis ball container
Large balloon
Rubber bands (2)
Eye Dropper
Water

Presentation:
1. Fill container almost full with water.
2. Fill eye dropper with enough water to keep all but the tip of the rubber head submerged.
3. Cut the neck off of the balloon.
4. Tightly cover container with balloon.
5. Secure tightly in place with rubber bands.
6. Press the balloon and watch the dropper drop.

Open Ended Question:
1. How did you make the dropper go down?

Notes:
If dropper becomes sluggish, adjust amount of water in the dropper.

Bubble Tank

Materials:

Tank/Aquarium
Water
Large Tubing
Straws (cut in half)
Objects: Bottles, flasks, plastic pipes, plastic pipe joints, cup with holes.

Presentation:

1. Fill tank with water.
2. Submerge objects.
3. Place end of tubing at the bottom of the tank.
4. Place one straw in the opposite end of tubing.
5. Tubing in tank should be moved from object to object.
6. Blow through straw so bubbles cause various effects.
7. Make sure children view the bubble action not only from above but from the side of the tank.

Open Ended Question:

1. What do the bubbles do to the flask? bottles? etc.
2. What are bubbles made of?
3. How can you move the bottles, flasks, etc.?

Variations:

1. Use different objects so bubble actions vary.

Balloon Pump

Materials: Old Windex bottle
                         Balloon

Presentation: 1. Secure balloon over mouth of bottle.
                         2. Squeeze bottle.
                         3. Balloon will inflate.

Racing Waters

Materials:

Colored water
Plastic cups
Straws
Clear plastic tubing

Presentation:

1. Fill cup with water
2. Cut straw in half.
3. Insert straw into one end of tubing.
4. Wrap the tubing around child, objects, etc.
5. Insert remaining end of tubing into colored water cup.
6. Instruct child to suck on straw to bring water through tubing.
7. Instruct child to blow on straw to push water back into cup.
8. Watch as water races through tubing.

Open Ended Question:

1. How can you make the water move?
2. What else can you do with the water?
3. Where else can you put the tubing?

Note:

1. For sanitary reasons, make sure each child has their own cup and straw.
2. Let the child know it is OK to swallow the water.

Airplane Launcher

Materials:
Duct tape
Old Windex bottle
Clay
Straw
Tube from a pen
Index card

Presentation:
1. Cover mouth of bottle with clay.
2. Insert pen tube through clay.
3. Secure clay around tube so half of pen tube is in the bottle and the rest is outside the bottle.
4. Poke straw through pen tube to remove any clay.
5. Remove straw.
6. Tape one end of straw closed.
7. Tape index card to closed end of straw so that it serves as wings.
8. Place remaining end of straw in pen tube.
9. Give a good hard squeeze to the bottle and the airplane will launch.

Open Ended Question:
1. What makes the airplane fly?
2. What happens when you squeeze the bottle?
3. How far can you make the airplane go?

Variations:
1. Attach various items to the straw for various effects.

Notes:
1. Make sure to point away from people and animal cages.

Fan Races

Materials:

Fan
Straws
Paper
Hole puncher
String

Presentation:

1. Cut 3 (5' to 6') pieces of string.
2. Tie one end of each piece of string on the fan close to the center of the fan.
3. Cut straws in half.
4. Punch a hole (in different spots) in 3 pieces of paper. (Paper should be sturdy and no larger than 5" x 5".)
5. Thread each straw through the hole in one of the pieces of paper.
6. Thread each piece of string through a straw.
7. Give each child the end of a piece of the string to hold. (If one child you may tie off the strings on a yard stick (see photo).
8. Pull straws back so they are touching the fan.
9. Turn the fan on and watch as the straws and paper race to the children.

Open Ended Questions:

1. What made the straws and paper move?
2. Which paper came to you first? Why?

Variations:

Replace the paper with paper airplanes, etc.

Notes:

Keep children away from fan blades.

Whirley Birds

Materials:

String
Clay
Tape
4 paper plates
Scissors
Straws

Presentation:

1. Cut 4 pieces of string to extend from the ceiling to the floor.
2. Secure one end of each piece of string to the ceiling.
3. Strings should be approximately 8" apart.
4. Punch a hole in the center of each plate.
5. Cut plate edges in a different pattern for each plate, i.e., (like a propeller, a wheel, etc.).
6. Cut the straws into 4 – 2" pieces.
7. Thread each plate through its center hole with a straw (straws should fit snugly in place).
8. Thread the unattached end of each piece of string through a straw and plate.
9. Now secure the string to the floor with tape and a lump of clay to keep the string taut.
10. Raise the plates, give them a spin, and watch them fall.

Open Ended Questions:

1. Which plate fell to the ground first?
2. How can you make plates spin?

Variations:

1. Increase the number of strings and plates.
2. Have plate races.
3. Decorate plates.

39

Water

Super Siphon

Materials:

2 pitchers or clear containers
Colored water
Large Plastic Tubing (7 ft. approx.)

Presentation:

1. Fill one pitcher with colored water.
2. Place the full pitcher at a higher level than the empty pitcher.
3. Put one end of the tubing into the full pitcher.
4. Put the other end of the tubing into the empty pitcher.
5. To begin the siphon effect, orally inhale through the tubing. This will draw the water to the empty pitcher.

Open Ended Question:

1. What makes the water move?
2. How did *you* make the water move from here (point to the empty pitcher to the new full pitcher) to there?

Variations:

1. The height of the full pitcher can be raised and lowered to vary water's travelling speed.

Magic Touching Bag

Materials:

Ziploc Plastic Bag
Corn Starch (5 tbs.)
Water (1/2 cup)
Oil (1/2 cup)
Green & Blue Food Coloring (2 drops each)

Presentation:

1. Combine corn starch, water, and food coloring in bag.
2. Mix ingredients.
3. Add oil to bag.
4. Seal the bag.
5. Lay flat on table.
6. Press ingredients w/finger.
7. Watch as colors mix and separate.

Open Ended Question:

1. What colors do you see?
2. How can you make the liquid move?

Variations:

1. Different food colorings.

Note:

For vigorous use: lay bag flat on table and cover with clear contact paper.
Contact paper should extend over the bag approx. 2 inches in each direction.

Run Away Powder

Materials:

Pie Pan
Talcum Powder
Water
Bar of Ivory Soap
Tempra Paint (if desired)

Presentation:

1. Fill pan with water.
2. Sprinkle enough talcum powder and tempra to cover the entire surface of the water.
3. Place bar of soap in the center of the pan.
4. Watch powder run away.

Open Ended Question:

1. How did you make the powder move?
2. What did the soap do to the powder?

Crazy Crayon Shavings

Materials: Large clear plastic bottle
                          Crayon shavings (multi-colored) (2 tbsp.)
                          Water

Presentation: 1. Fill bottle with water and crayon shavings.
                          2. Seal bottle.
                          3. Shake bottle or move in a circular motion for a tornado effect.

Open Ended Question: 1. What makes the shavings move?
                          2. How else can you make them move?

Note: Large and long crayon shavings work best.

Oil & Water Drop Painting

Materials:

Paper   Water
Tray   2 eye droppers
Cooking oil   2 contrasting colors of tempra paint (powder)

Presentation:

1. Mix one color paint with oil.
2. Mix another color paint with water.
3. Place paper in tray.
4. Using first eye dropper, drop water paint onto paper.
5. Using second eye dropper, drop oil paint on top of water paint.
6. Rock pan back and forth for desired effect.
7. Oil color will float on top of water color creating unique effect.

Open Ended Question:

1. Why don't the colors mix?

Variations:

1. Vary colors of paint.
2. Vary size of paper and tray.
3. Vary amounts of colors.

Rivers and Canals

Materials:

Plastic drop cloth (throwaway kind)
Water Source
Water Play Canals (optional)
Plastic boats
Shovels
Pails

Presentation:

1. Show children how the drop cloth can be used for construction of rivers and canals.
2. Give the children the remaining materials.

Open Ended Questions:

1. What can you make with these things?
2. How did you make the water move?

Variations:

1. Include additional items, i.e., rope and boards.

Bubble Machine

Materials:

Water play tub or clear tank
Fish tubing
Straws
Sharp pointed nail
Duct tape
Water

Presentation:

1. In a completely dry tub tape down fish tubing (serpentine style).
2. Leave approx. 4" inches of tubing over the edge of the tub on either side.
3. Cut numerous small holes into tubing.
4. Fill tank with water.
5. Put half of the straws on either end of the exposed tubing.
6. Allow children to blow on straws.
7. Hundreds of bubbles will noisily make their way to the surface.

Open Ended Questions:

1. What do you see?
2. What do you hear?
3. How do they feel? (Put hand in tank while blowing.)

Variations:

1. Color the water.

Fountain Towers

Materials:

4 old plastic tempra paint jars
Water play tub
Hammer and 1 nail
Water

Presentation:

1. Fill 1 jar with water and place in tub.
2. Make two holes very low on the sides of the jar. They should be directly across from each other. Use hammer and nail (see photo).
3. Make 3 holes in the 3rd jar (in approx. equal distances apart).
4. Make 4 holes in the 4th jar (in approx equal distances apart).
5. Fill 2nd jar with water and place on first.
6. Fill 3rd jar with water and place on 2nd.
7. Fill 4th jar with water and place on 3rd.
8. Watch as towering jars turn into a fountain.

Open Ended Questions:

1. How does the water come out of the jars?
2. What makes the fountain stop?
3. What makes it go again.

Variations:

1. Color the water.
2. Make a hole in the <u>bottom</u> of jars 2, 3 and 4. This keeps the fountain running continuously. You need only continue to fill the top jar.

Ice Caverns

Materials:
Large piece of ice (freeze in large mixing bowl the night before)
Salt
Food coloring
Warm water
Ziploc bags
Tray
Scissors

Presentation:
1. In a Ziploc bag, mix 1/4 cup of warm water, 15 drops of food coloring and 3/4 cups of salt.
2. Seal bag and shake ingredients.
3. Place ice in a tray.
4. Pour a cup of water over ice to make it slick.
5. Hold bag at an angle so liquid gathers at one lower corner.
6. Hold bag (similar to holding a cake icing bag) (see photo).
7. With scissors, snip a small hole at the tip of the bag so liquid will squirt out.
8. Allow children to squirt small amounts of mixture onto ice. (Try not to let too much mixture pile up in one area — if it does, rinse with a little water.)
9. Watch as small cracks and caverns begin to form.

Open Ended Questions:
1. What is happening to the ice.

Variations:
1. Vary sizes of ice.
2. Vary colors and consistencies of salt/food coloring.

Notes:
Make sure to make at least 2 colors of mixture bags for color contrast. More depending on size of ice.

Sand Box Plumbing

Materials:
Plastic pipe and joints
Funnel
Water source
Buckets
Sand box area

Presentation:
1. Supply children with the above materials.
2. Allow them to construct pipeworks.

Open Ended Questions:
1. How did you get the water from here to there?
2. How can you make the water move a different way?

Notes:
Some two- and three-year-olds are more fascinated with pouring the water in and watching it come out than the actual construction of the pipes. Teachers or older children may assist in construction development.

Clean Water Machine

Materials:
Glass jar
Clear plastic funnel or clear vinyl
Sand
Gravel
Water
Salt
Clear measuring cup

Presentation:
1. Fill the funnel or vinyl (if vinyl — fold in cone shape leaving a small hole at the tip) 1/4 of the way full with clean gravel.
2. Fill in an additional 1/4 with **clean** sand.
3. Fill in an additional 1/4 with gravel again.
4. Fill clear measuring cup with water.
5. Muddy the water with a little soil.
6. Slowly pour muddied water into the funnel/vinyl.
7. Watch as water that exits the funnel/vinyl is clear.

Open Ended Questions:
1. What happened to the muddy water?
2. What does the sand and gravel do?

Power Stream

Materials:

Plastic tempra paint jar w/lid
Eye dropper
Nail and hammer
Scissors
Plastic/rubber tubing
Water

Presentation:

1. Remove lid from paint jar.
2. Punch nail through the lid with hammer.
3. Remove nail.
4. Remove rubber part of eye dropper.
5. Put one blade of scissors into the hole in the lid.
6. Twist the scissors to form a hole just a little smaller than the eye dropper.
7. Insert eye dropper into hole with its small end pointing out of the jar.
8. Secure tubing over large end of eye dropper.
9. Tubing should hang about 1/4" from the bottom of the paint jar when the lid is screwed on.
10. Fill the paint jar 3/4s full of water.
11. Put the lid on the paint jar.
12. Give the bottle a squeeze and a stream of water will shoot up.

Open Ended Questions:

1. What did you do to the water?
2. How high can you make the water go?

Variations:

1. Secure cut straws over the tip of the eye dropper (while lid is securely on paint jar) and have children blow into the paint jar. (Water will shoot back out.)
2. Set up targets to try and hit with the water stream.

Notes:

This is a wet activity and works well outdoors.

Light

Shadow Play

Materials: Film or slide projector
White background (wall, sheet, butcher paper)
Props: Dramatic figures of all kinds, i.e., dinosaurs, dolls, bodies, heads, hands, etc.

Presentation:
1. Set up projector to make a light square of at least 4' x 4'.
2. Experiment with placement of objects between projector and screen (i.e., sharp dark shadows and soft fuzzy ones).
3. Shadows will come to life as children begin to play.

Open Ended Question:
1. How did you make your shadow on the screen?
2. What else can you make on the screen?

Variations:
1. Use colored cellophane to project a colored screen.
2. Use music or background sounds, and story tapes for dramatic play.

Sun Tag

Materials: Sunny day
                        Small mirror, i.e., old compact mirrors, etc.

Presentation: 1. Show children how a reflection works from the sun to the mirror to
                           another object.
                        2. Show them how to tag one another with the reflection.
                        3. Supply each child with a mirror.
                        4. Sun tag will begin.

Open Ended Questions: 1. How did you make a reflection?
                          2. What can you make the reflection do?
                          3. How can you move the reflection?

Variations: 1. Use different sizes of mirrors.
                        2. Have children try to catch the reflection.
                        3. Supply child with two mirrors at the same time.

Star Box

Materials:

Large cardboard box
Hammer and 1 nail
Cloth
Black paint
Duct tape

Presentation:

1. Turn box so open end faces up.
2. Duct tape down any flaps on the inside of the box.
3. Have children paint the inside of the box black.
4. Beginning at the top edge of one side of the box, cut a semicircle large enough for a child's midsection.
5. Attach a piece of cloth over the hole so no light can enter the box (see photo).
6. With hammer and nail make numerous holes all over the box. (The holes can vary from pinhole size to nailhead size.
7. Place box in a sunny or well lit room.
8. Allow children to lie down inside the box.

Open Ended Question:

1. What do you see?
2. Tell me about where you are?

Variations:

1. Punch holes in the form of constellations.
2. Paint planets with glow in the dark paint.
3. Create a sound tape to go with the stargazing.

Notes:

Children can do this entire project with little to no teacher guidance.

Slide Show

Materials:

Black paint or marker
Small box (4" x 1-1/2" or slide size)
Slide
Tape
Scissors

Presentation:

1. Remove one of the small sides of the box.
2. Paint or color the inside of the box black.
3. Tape the slide over the open end of the box so that no openings remain.
4. Take the end of the box opposite the slide and poke a hole in it. The hole should be no larger than 1/8".
5. Point the slide end of box toward the light and look through the hole.
6. Now you can view a slide show.

Open Ended Question:

1. Tell me what you see?

Variations:

1. Supply numerous boxes with slides.
2. Supply slides of children of classroom themes.

Starry Night

Materials:
Dark blue paper (approx. 3' x 4')
Dark blue tissue paper (approx 3' x 3')
Nail
Tape

Presentation:
1. Secure paper with tape across an open space (i.e., puppet theater or doorway.
2. Punch holes of varying sizes all over paper. (Holes should be no larger than a nail head.)
3. Place tissue over entire paper.
4. Tape tissue in place.
5. Set up projector behind paper (not tissue side).
6. Adjust light to cover paper's dimensions.
7. Darken room and behold a beautiful sky.

Open Ended Questions:
1. Tell me about what you see?
2. When have you seen something like this before?

Variations:
1. Make holes in the patterns of constellations.
2. Use audio tapes to enhance the atmosphere.

Thank you...

Diane, Carmen, Ligaya,
Lisa, Louise, J.P., Matt, Leslie, Wes
and all the children from
the Early Learning Center.

Resource List

Radio Shack
100 One Tandy Center
Fort Worth, TX 76102
(Small motors)
(Call for the location nearest you)

Tap Plastics
6475 Sierra Lane
Dublin, CA 94568
(Plexiglass, clear acrylic tubes)

Creative Educational Surplus
1588 S. Victoria Road
Mendota Heights, MN 55118
(All sorts of neat, cheap stuff!)

Local Hardware
or Plumbing store
(Plastic pipe and joints,
plastic tubing, springs, washers,
and nuts, etc.)

National Association for
the Education of Young Children
1834 Connecticut Avenue N.W.
Washington, D.C. 20009
(Developmentally appropriate
practice guidelines)

ORDER FORM

Receive your own copy of *Wonderscience!*

Please complete the following form and enclose a check or money order payable to:

Learning Expo Publishing
5420 S. Espana Ct.
Aurora, CO 80015

Quantity:

_____ Wonderscience **$14.95 per book** _____

Colorado residents add local sales tax. _____

Freight $3.00 per book in U.S.A. _____

Total _____

Mailing label:

From: Learning Expo Publishing
5420 S. Espana Ct.
Aurora, CO 80015

To: Name: _____

Address: _____

City, State, Zip: _____

Science Notes